A VISION OF **EXCELLENCE**
Getting Back Up

GREG GOODMAN, SR.

A VISION OF **EXCELLENCE**
Getting Back Up

GREG GOODMAN, SR.

MISSION POSSIBLE PRESS

MISSION POSSIBLE PRESS
Creating Legacies through Absolute Good Works

The Mission is Possible.

Sharing love and wisdom for the young and "the young at heart," expanding minds, restoring kindness through good thoughts, feelings, and attitudes is our intent. May you thrive and be good in all you are and all you do...

Be Cause U.R. Absolute Good!

A Vision of Excellence © 2019 by Greg Goodman, Sr.

No part of this book may be reproduced in any written, electronic, recording, or photocopying form without written permission of the publisher. The exception would be in the case of brief quotations embodied in critical articles or reviews and pages where permission is specifically granted by the publisher.

Although every precaution has been taken to verify the accuracy of the information contained herein, the author and publisher assume no responsibility for any errors or omissions. No liability is assumed for damages that may result from the use of information contained within. All rights reserved worldwide.

Books may be purchased in quantity by contacting the publisher directly:

Mission Possible Press, A division of Absolute Good,
PO Box 8039 St. Louis, MO 63156
or by calling 240.644.2500
MissionPossiblePress.com

ISBN: 978-0-9996766-5-3

First Edition   Printed in the United States

Dedication

To my son, Gregory Goodman, Jr., the first time I laid eyes on you, you had my heart. God called you home at 9 years old and I miss you more every day. Everything I do today is to make you proud to call me your dad. May you Rest In Peace, son.

To my daughters, Jennifer and Tiffanie, you are both beautiful, responsible young women and I'm proud and overjoyed to be your dad. Looking forward to witnessing your bright futures!

Acknowledgements

Special thanks to my mother for always believing in me. Thanks to my dad, Gerald J. Cox Sr., for influencing my life in so many ways. May you Rest in Peace.

Also thanks to all my siblings who over the years have always shown me unconditional love. Finally thanks to my publisher and writing coach Jo Lena Johnson, I couldn't have done this without you.

Contents

1) Growing Up in Gary 1
2) Getting High 5
3) Germany Blew My Mind 9
4) Exiting the Army and Our Marriage 13
5) Crack in the Kitchen 15
6) Losing My Son 19
7) 2001 29
8) Budgeting Addictions 35
9) Getting Past the Fear 41
10) Looking Into the Mirror 45
11) Are You Due for A Change? 53
12) About the Author 59

Growing Up in Gary

I'm the oldest of five children – three girls and two boys. My earliest memory is when we lived in the Ivanhoe Projects, which they've since torn down, in my hometown of Gary, Indiana. We lived in a unit which had five apartments connected to each other and the rooms were very small. And even at that young age, I knew we were poor when I told people where I lived, based on the way they responded. It was embarrassing. When the neighbors had roaches, we had roaches. That's the way it was. And the neighbors had roaches. My dad moved us into a house when I was around five years old.

Moving from the projects to a house showed me we could live in a house – and showed me that life could be different – that I could make significant changes. I thought we were rich. New school, new clothes, my own room, downstairs, big backyard, a dog. We had cherry and berry trees in our yard and lived next door to white people. My dad worked in the steel mill as we then grew up middle class. My parents were married for 14 years. We had a two-parent household until they divorced. Then my mom raised us by herself.

My dad, who was an only child, was a pretty strict disciplinarian. He passed away at 50 years old. I looked at him as being a tough guy but smoking cigarettes and breathing in all the air from the steel mill may have affected him. A lot of what I do and what I got came from him.

I Was Upset When I learned the Truth

My mother's mother didn't like the way my dad was disciplining me, feeling he was too strict. One day, when I was around 12, I was complaining about his treatment and she as a grandmother, took my side out of love, as opposed to taking into consideration that I was a young man growing up in Gary. In her attempts to try and make me feel better, she told me that he wasn't my biological father. I immediately wondered why my mother hadn't told me. Each of my other siblings were his, but I was the oldest. He had come into my life when I was a one year old. When I heard that, it crushed me. Had I been told that he wasn't my biological father, and that I had to follow his rules because I was living under his roof, that would have helped me understand. He was taking care of me, and he was preparing me to be a man. If I understood those things it would have helped our relationship. Nothing was the same after I found out the truth. I already had an independent spirit and then when I found out he wasn't my dad, it gave me license to say certain things and have a different attitude. That was all bad. I wish she hadn't told me.

Statements like, "You're not my dad," came out of my mouth and I had that stance. It helped me to feel bold and be rebellious. As an adult, a grown man, even though he's long since passed he's still my dad. I'm just glad that though he wasn't perfect, he loved me and I loved him. I'm grateful that he showed me that we could move from the projects to a house and to see myself as a man. That he taught me I could work hard and learn the things I needed and deserved. He taught me that although your actions may not always appear to be loving, they may not always be kind. You can change. Of course, I had to learn a lot of things the hard way.

Later in life he, my father, my dad, and I had a good relationship. But it happened after I became a man. I had to recognize who he was and how his actions and behaviors shaped me. I thought about why he behaved the way he did. I don't think he was a bad guy. He was an only child who grew up without his father in the home. His mom was very strict and he learned how to function and take care of business. But for whatever reasons some of his actions ended up being abusive. Perhaps that was based on his own childhood experiences? After I became a man we continued to talk and our relationship evolved. He helped me out a lot.

So, I'm grateful to my dad for the things he said and did although he made it harder on himself and on us at times. But looking back, so did I.

Getting High

"Smoking weed was cool, but I didn't know how much it would change my life."

The first time I got high was the summer before my freshman year at Lew Wallace High School in Gary. I was 14 years old and I was hanging with some older male relatives who were weed smokers. At some point I asked them to pass it to me and I got high with them. It was everything I thought it was going to be. I was hooked.

My relatives were my source since I didn't have a job. Soon after that experience, and before school started, I started working, delivering newspapers. I didn't make a lot of money but it gave me some extra change in my pocket to buy lunch and to "put five on it" when I started making my own connects. Back then you could get a nickel bag of weed, which was the equivalent of ten joints. That was a good deal! I would go to the arcade/carryout restaurant around the corner from Grandmother's house all the time. Going there helped me to meet people who were connected to the folks who sold the weed. Before the summer was over, I made my direct connections to my own supplier. That was a busy, good summer for me.

By the time school started, my friend Brian had an older girlfriend who had already graduated. Sometimes I would skip class and go over her house with them. I could do whatever I wanted while I was there. It was fun, cool, made the day go by faster and it made me feel good.

I began getting high before school. I had algebra first period. Instead of catching the bus to school, I would walk because I knew I could get high on my way. Sometimes I was by myself, sometimes I was with other kids. I really like math and I'm good at it. The first marking period I was focused, doing well. I got an A. I was like, "I got this." By the end of the second marking period my grade had slipped to a B. I was losing focus because I was getting high. By the end of the school year, I was getting high on a regular basis, and whenever I could. I ended up with an F in the last marking period because by that time I was skipping my classes. Even then, I think that had to do with not wanting to go into class smelling like weed. I didn't want to be labeled as "that guy" everyone knows smokes weed. So it was easier to not be present than to be "him." In my mind, I was thinking at that time that it was cool and it made me feel like I was more of an adult than everyone else in the 9th grade. Once I attached smoking weed to being cool, that made it alright for me. But my grades really told the truth.

By the end of my freshman year, Mom made a decision that enough was enough. She showed me her strength and her point of no return. She did have the power to end the abuse by leaving however, she took it for us kids. That taught me perseverance and showed me sacrifice, though I didn't get it at the time.

During my sophomore year, I was taking two lunch hours, skipping typing class and failing my easy ROTC class – not going meant failing. My mom didn't know I was skipping. She never got any calls nor did she go up to the school. When she saw my grades, she would tell me I could do better than that. She knew I was smart but she didn't know why my grades were so bad. She probably has some of my report cards now.

My son was born during my junior year so that made it a little different as far as money goes. At that point I was working at a grocery store and they were paying me under the table. If I was going to buy weed or buy pampers, that was a decision I had to make. I wasn't smoking as much because I was on a high because of my son and I made the effort to be responsible. I also didn't want to go around him smelling like weed.

During my senior year, I was trying to figure out what I was going to do. His mom became his sole provider, as she was getting assistance. I fell back into my routine and picked up my old habits. At home, my mom was enforcing rules I thought were too strict and I didn't want to deal with that. I felt like I was grown since I had a kid. But my mother was like, "You may be feeling that way but you aren't grown here." I moved about 35 miles away to Michigan City with my grandmother and changed schools. I know my mother didn't want me to move, but I'm glad she let me. When that happened, I met some different people in the school who always had connections to weed. I didn't have a job but I was just cool with the people who had it, so I just started the same routine. Then some of my relatives had friends who would also share. It worked out. Whenever I had money I would contribute.

I didn't have a car but I would go back and forth to Gary once or twice a month when I could catch a ride and see my girlfriend, my son, and my mom. I was always going to see my mom no matter what.

Army Bound

I graduated, and on time, but I had no skills. However, I knew I had to get serious since I had to take care of my little family. I gave myself a "clean period" from the weed toward the end of the school year. I graduated in May and was on my way to the Army in June. My basic training was in Fort Sill, Oklahoma for 13 weeks. When I graduated, I came home at the end of October, turned 19 November 6th, married my girlfriend on November 8th, and was sent to Amberg, Germany on November 9th, where I was stationed for 2 ½ years.

> *"Being a soldier was the end of my getting high, or so I thought."*

Germany Blew My Mind

"Dippin' and dappin', trying to find out what's happenin'. I entered the country clean, with high hopes."

Newly married, I was a dedicated soldier, committed to being a good husband and a responsible father to my toddler. I was there for the first six months by myself and got everything set up for my family. Then my wife, who was six months pregnant, arrived with my son. During my first year in Amberg, I did not touch any drugs, as I didn't want to risk it and fail any random drug tests.

Hash

I started going out with some of the other soldiers. They weren't smoking weed but they were smoking hash. I didn't know anything about it, and had never heard of hash before. I was hesitant and scared to try it. I knew what would happen if I failed a drug test. I would have to pay a fine for three months, have to do 45 days of extra duty, I would get demoted to the lowest rank in addition to taking a pay cut because of the demotion, and I would have to go to rehab classes. I didn't have time for none of that.

But they convinced me to try it because they had a way of passing the drug test if we had any randoms. I decided I would try it. Since they had the connections, I would just give them the money and they would get it. It was something new and different but at the end of the day, it was still just a high. I think it was the excitement of being in a foreign place and I could still get high, though I was in a military environment. I think I also got off on feeling like a 20 year old daredevil, since I had the pills I could take, in case I came up for testing. My wife never knew and I never got caught. I guess the pills worked.

Partying Like I Was Single

I think it was the age and that I was in another country, excited about my surroundings that had me acting like I was single. I started hanging out a lot more, going different places, and then had my own connections, which meant I didn't have to divvy up or share. There were people who had different gambling parties and I enjoyed participating. Though I was in another country, these activities made me feel comfortable, as if I was at home. I never went back to the U.S. on leave because my family was there with me and I didn't have the extra money. I wasn't responsible with the money. In some aspects, I think I was still trying to live a single lifestyle at that time. So not only was I getting high regularly and gambling, but we also had our second child. It was all bad.

Even buying hash was always a risk – being in a foreign country, I would get some batches which weren't as good as before. It wasted money but it didn't stop me. I was trying to be low-key since I was in the military but since these were Germans we were buying it from, it's not like I could go and report bad product. Ultimately my activities jeopardized our living and lifestyle. Our phone got disconnected. I was paying bills late, including the rent and it just put a lot of unnecessary stress on our relationship.

Stress in our marriage and my life, in my mind, was more of a reason to just do it – to get high. *In this moment I'll get high and I don't have to worry about what's going on over at the house.* It's my break away. Mentally, I think that's where the habit starts to form, escaping stress and "using" as a form of stress relief. Once I locked that thought in my mind that the high would be my escape that thought followed me. I wasn't thinking, *When I come down from the high, the stress is still going to be here.* In those moments when I anticipated being high, any other thoughts went away.

About a month before I was to get out of the military we had a big argument because of me going out partying. My response? I went out to party to get away from the argument. She didn't want me to go. I got pulled over by the German Police and I was buzzed – we had been drinking and smoking. It was all bad. They called the military police, and they came and got me. They restricted me to post and three weeks later I was back in the U.S., as the government paid for me to get back to the states but they wouldn't pay for my family to do so. They paid for her to come over but they weren't paying for her to get back since I was not processing to another station, and was exiting the Army.

"Just like the hash, that policy blew my mind."

Exiting the Army and Our Marriage

"A continental divide separated us."

My wife and children were in Germany, needing to get back to the states but I was mad and didn't help her to get back to the States. After all of my going out, acting single, seeing other people and partying, she was frustrated and started going out acting single as well, to my surprise. The person who took me to the airport revealed her activities to me and I was pissed. We were both 22 and acting like immature adults, which we were. After I found out what she had been doing, I refused to pay for her and the kids to get out of Germany.

Her mother paid for her and the kids to get back to the U.S. a couple of weeks after I arrived back in the states.

The only reason I felt bad about it was because I had left the kids, because they were innocent and had nothing to do with anything. Emotionally I was hurt even though I was cheating, I couldn't handle the thought of her doing the same thing. The thought of leaving my kids there put me in a bad space, and that stayed with me for a long time.

I still ended my military service with an honorable discharge, something which didn't have to happen because I had gotten detained. They just processed me out and didn't put it on my record. As I look back, there's no way I should have walked away with no consequences. It was truly a blessing.

Once my family returned to the States we tried to reconcile our relationship and moved into an apartment together. I worked as a cashier at a truck stop and though I occasionally smoked weed, I didn't have to have it, I just liked getting high. She was working at a meat packing plant and we were struggling to raise our little children with the small amount of income we made and with the damage which had been done during our marriage. We stayed together about a year but it was heartbreaking. Not only did I try and rebuild with my wife, I also had to rebuild with my son. He had started calling me Mr. Goodman instead of Dad. I had a lot of making up to do. But the damage was done and the trust was lost. We decided it would be best to separate, and did so in early 1990.

In October 1991, I got a job as a Correctional Officer at a maximum control facility outside of Gary. It took nearly two years for our divorce to be final, but once it was, in 1992, our children were eight and five. During the separation and pending divorce I was grateful for the continuing support of her family, which made the transition easier.

> *"If I would have been stateside I think I would have done 20 years in the military. That six months of partying I did before they arrived in Germany wasn't a good start for a solid marriage."*

Crack in the Kitchen

"I came prepared for the party, but she had something else cooking."

After the separation, my family moved to my mother-in-law's house and I stayed in the apartment. During that summer (1990) I was at a shopping mall and I saw this fine, brown-skinned young woman with a nice shape and a pretty face walking toward me. As she was passing by, I spoke to her and she smiled. I struck up a conversation and she told me she was having a get-together at her house the next day and asked if I wanted to come. Of course I said yes. Later that night we talked on the phone. During our conversation we talked about playing cards, drinking and smoking weed, so of course, I was prepared when I got to her house, weed in hand.

I was the first to arrive. Her apartment was nice, clean and I felt comfortable as I sat down at the kitchen table. At first I didn't pay attention to the boiling pot on the stove but when she turned the stove off and put the contents into a glass of water, I knew what it was. She had boiled cocaine and turned it into crack. I was hesitant about it because I was a weed smoker only, but she was fine. She was going to lace the weed with the crack, making "primo" joints. At that point I had to make a decision – and I did. I knew, if that's what she was doing, that's what I was doing too.

We rolled and smoked a primo joint together. Afterward I went into the living room and sat on the couch. My head was spinning. I had never been that high before. I don't even remember when the other people came in. I didn't like the feeling because I felt like I didn't have control over myself. *I can't wait to leave. I'm never doing this again,* is what I remember thinking.

Once I was able to gather myself I told her I was leaving, and did so. I wasn't mad at her. I had made the decision to indulge and I did. But it was time to go.

"I went back to just smoking plain old weed and was quite fine with that. After that experience I was done with crack, or so I thought."

I've never been a follower, I actually pride myself on choosing what I'm going to do and how I'm going to do it. Looking back today, I can say that. But the reality is that I was an addict and enjoyed being high. Weed was good but by the Spring of 1992, I had been enjoying the habit for many years.

One of my co-workers invited me to a weekend party. When I arrived I smelled the distinctive smell of weed laced with crack. It wasn't what I was expecting but at that moment, I knew what it was going to be. I indulged that night and it felt all good, though it was really all bad.

I was addicted to the feeling and to the taste of smoking primos, and though I couldn't have predicted it that night, I would not be satisfied with smoking weed-only again.

> *"After that party, crack became part of my day-to-day living."*

Losing My Son

"Rebuilding with my son, despite the relationship with his mom was so important yet, at the time, I had no idea how important it was."

My mother-in-law, Ms. Brown, played a significant role in keeping our small family connected. I was invited to the family functions because of the relationship she and I had. I wasn't just a son-in-law or former son-in-law, I was accepted and treated like a son. To this day, we still have an amazing, loving relationship. She's a double amputee – she had five surgeries and I was there for each of them except one. My ex-wife and I were not on good terms when we actually divorced but with the type of relationship we had, it was never an issue going to get our children or picking them up. We always agreed as to when we would share time with the children.

Fatherhood

Initially because I was so young when my son was born, I wasn't ready for a family, yet I had one. But, because my own biological father had abandoned me, I definitely wasn't going to be apart from my kids. I was never going to be that absentee dad. Though I paid child support for them, I didn't just leave it at that. A lot of dads feel like as long as they pay that support, they've done their part, and the relationship is left out. Right after we separated I was trying to balance work, partying and spending time with my kids. In the beginning, I would choose partying over going to spend time with them. Part of that was because of my emotional immaturity, ego, and dislike that my ex had a boyfriend. The sad truth I wasn't seeing was that I had caused most of the issues, she got caught up.

I tried to compensate for me and their mom not being together by buying material things. I knew I couldn't get back the time that was lost but I knew that buying my children things would let them know that I loved and really cared about them. They may not have looked at it like I was just trying to make up for anything that had happened. They just probably thought dad was just buying them things and that made them happy. I would try to make things special for them, even going to their school on their birthdays, hosting little parties for them and their classmates. When I was in school, I saw parents do that and I promised myself I would do that with my own kids.

Whenever I did go to pick them up, they were so excited to spend time with me, especially Lil' Greg. The divorce gave me a chance to see myself, my past actions and to also make decisions about the type of father I would be moving forward. When I put things into perspective, I made sure to spend more quality time with my son. Rebuilding our relationship was important to me, and I was committed to it. Each time I reassured him that he was my first child, my only son and that I loved him unconditionally. He loved me so much that he easily let go of what happened in Germany. Kids are really something. It took me many, many years to get over my guilt of what happened there but he was happy go lucky and was excited just to be with me, no matter what we were doing.

When I saw him he would ask me if they were coming back to live with me. I would tell him that they had to stay with their mom because at that time, I didn't have my own place. He wanted to be with me, and he looked just like me. *I'm smiling and sad as I say that, missing him.* When I would go to the barbershop I would take him with me. He wore glasses like I did, and he looked like I spit him out. He was a great big brother for his sister. I let him know he had to take care of her, and he did. He was a smart kid. He didn't like living without me there or having another person in the house who was a father-figure, he told me several times he wished he could stay with me. By this time his mom had gotten into a serious relationship after our divorce and they were all living together. I let him know that he just had one dad. I was his dad and that was it. But I didn't want to cause any drama or friction for his mother. I told him that as long as the guy wasn't doing anything to hurt him, he had to listen to him.

Friday, July 8, 1994

I picked up the kids and we went to my mom's house. My daughter Jennifer was sleeping so Lil' Greg, who was nine at the time, and I went to the laundromat to wash clothes.

He asked me if they could spend the weekend with me. I had plans that weekend and told him no, but that they could stay with me the following weekend. I'm sure he was disappointed but he knew I would keep my word and come back and get them the following weekend.

Sunday, July 10, 1994

I didn't know at the time but his mom's family had planned a gathering at Miller Beach in Gary. My kids went, along with other relatives including his cousin, Ernest Jr., who was 11 at the time. While the rest of the family was in the picnic area, they allowed Greg and Ernest to go to the playground area, a few hundred feet away and they told them not to go to the beach or near the water.

That afternoon I got a frantic phone call from my mom, telling me to come to Methodist Hospital because Greg had been in an accident. When I got to the hospital I asked what had happened and his mom came and told me that they went to the water despite being told not to, and when they were called to eat, they didn't respond. She went to look for them and saw Lil' Greg in the water. She jumped in to try and save him. But the current and the undertow were too much. There were no life guards and when the rescue team arrived on the scene they found them together. Ernest Jr. at the other hospital, Mercy, had already been pronounced dead.

I was upset. I knew that if I would have told him not to go to the water, he would not have gone in. My mom was trying to calm me down as I was yelling for the doctor. When the doctor came toward me, I could see past him, Lil' Greg, through the opening in the curtain. He told me that they were trying to bring up his temperature with a heating blanket and my response to that was, "If my son and his cousin were in the water the same amount of time, how was one pronounced dead and the other one not?" I was starting to think they were wasting time, because I wanted someone to do something and not leave him back there by himself. I was asking my mom why they weren't doing something. Nobody had any answers.

At that moment I knew it was time to get high. I knew my son was dead and I knew my next step was to go and get high. *Come on and tell me my son is dead so I can go.* It was no sense in wasting time anymore. The head nurse and the doctor came back and wanted to take us to the quiet room. And we knew what they were going to say.

They said they did all they could do and he didn't make it. His mom fell down on the floor, my sister was screaming and I was just ready to go. I asked if I could go see him.

They said, "Sure, you can go see him." I went into the room and as I was looking at him, I was looking at myself – the spitting image of me – and I started rubbing my hand through his hair. I told him, "I'm sorry that I didn't let you stay with me for the weekend. I'm sorry I left you in Germany. I'm sorry that you couldn't live with me."

It was surreal. I had to believe it because I was standing there looking at him. It wasn't a dream. I started asking God why He didn't do something because I know He could have done something to save both of them. I could see out of my peripheral vision, my mom outside of the curtain. Then I heard her voice telling me it was time to let him go. I don't know why but as I was about to turn and leave, a mixture of water and blood came from his nose. At that point I lost it. I didn't know what to think. I was just somewhere else in my head.

We left the hospital. We left him there, in that little room, behind that curtain, alone.

I wasn't trying to think about what we had to do or arrangements we had to make. Though I knew what we had to do. I just needed to leave. I needed to get high.

When I left the hospital I went straight to the drug house and spent $100 on crack and weed. I sat in my car, by myself, getting high. Afterward, I went home and couldn't sleep. I knew I was going to have to pull myself together and manage the arrangements of burying my son. That week was surreal, painful and full of harsh realities. Not only were we grieving, I was dealing with the anger and shame of feeling like I had let my son down, feeling that had I been there, he would still be alive. When I found out that my job only gave $2,000 in death benefits, I was overcome and even more overwhelmed. *How could my son's life be valued so low?*

The funeral was scheduled for Friday and everything was in place to send my little man out in style. I was sensitive, hurt and upset with God and everyone else. The only reason I was able to stay calm was because I knew I had to get those arrangements complete.

Thursday Night, July 14, 1994

I called my friend Chris and asked him to come hang out with me. With all of the arrangements complete, knowing I had to bury my son the next morning I wanted to escape the fear, the dread, the emotion and the reality of what had happened and what was about to happen.

We went to the park, smoked, sat and I let go of my feelings for a couple of hours. The crack helped me do that.

On my way home from the park I had a break down. It could have been a crack-induced break down or it may have been my emotions boiling over, but it was a breakdown nonetheless. Before that moment I had suppressed everything I had been feeling but I lost it. I was on the side of the road sobbing uncontrollably for a good while. It was the first time and only time in my life I had felt that way. In my great angst I questioned God and everything I had known, including myself. A father is not supposed to bury his son.

Friday Morning, July 15, 1994

We had a double funeral. We honored Gregory Goodman, Jr. and Ernest Wilson Jr., together. It was sadder than one could imagine. Looking at our boys, side by side, facing them and their open caskets, struggling to say our final goodbyes. Before I would see my son for the last time, I placed each of the four Teenage Mutant Ninja Turtles in his casket, as they had been his favorite. The boys were buried next to each other in the cemetery. As we left in the procession, we were all quiet. Silence filled the car as we each processed and considered how we were to live our lives with the huge void the children had left. My ex-wife went to her mom's house and took our daughter, Jennifer with her. I went to my mom's house and sat outside with my sister, listening to music, as several of my old friends came to check on me. It was a painful, solemn and quiet night.

When I returned to work that Monday, I focused on work and tried to get back to normal. But what did normal actually mean? I was in a prison, guarding prisoners, and trying desperately, not to allow the pain to overcome me again. It's all I could really do. I was just back to work, not really anything else.

I Wondered What God's Message Was For Me

The first thing I had to try to come to grips with was that I was thankful that both of my kids didn't drown that day. Instead of him and his cousin, it could have been him and his sister, my daughter Jennifer. I had to wrap my mind around that.

I was grieving and went through all of those stages and emotions. I told myself and God I wasn't going to get high anymore. I wanted to live a better life. I told myself I would no longer smoke weed mixed with crack. I told myself I would make it. I wanted to die, but I had to live. I didn't know how I was going to live but told myself I would live without getting high.

"I had the best intentions, but my ability to stop getting high was overcome by my addiction."

2001

"Here one minute, gone the next."

My addiction caused me to misplace priorities and relationships. In 2001, seven years after I lost my son, I also lost two other important people in my life.

Even though I called myself being a functional addict, it was hard to juggle life and being addicted. Since I had a job I was able to take care of my habit on my own and still function. However, many people are not able to do that because being an addict takes money. And if the sole priority is getting high, then all of the other activities revolve around that. Some people end up burning bridges, committing crimes to feed the habit, and don't even try to get a job. I would say that could be called "being relentless" because feeding the addiction is their sole priority over everything. In other words, being a non-functioning addict, if there is such a thing, really. The way I "functioned" as an addict, I wouldn't classify my behavior as relentless per se, but I would say I was extremely selfish and didn't put my loved ones first when I could or should have, choosing the high over them.

My Dad Died in May

I saw him before he went into the hospital and we had a few good conversations. I even went and took care of some personal business for him. However, the day he called from his bed, I didn't answer because I was likely high. His message said, "I'd like to see my son." I didn't call him back. The next call was from my sister, saying, "Dad has passed." When I went to the house, because I lived so close, I was the first to see his body. I called my mom and then the authorities. I didn't want my siblings to see Dad like that – on the floor, with one sock on and one sock off, fully dressed otherwise – so I wouldn't let them enter the house. They came into the house after the coroners took him out. After all of that, I went and got high with a friend.

In November My Fiancé Passed

When my youngest daughter, Tiffanie, was three years old in 2001, I was engaged to Toi but still living with my daughter and her mom, Donna. It was messy.

The night my fiancé died, I talked to her on the phone when she was getting ready for work and I had just gotten high… I made a decision not to go to her house that night and she said she didn't care whether I came or not because she was getting ready for work. My daughter's mother woke me up around 6 o'clock the next morning and told me Toi was dead, that she had died in a car accident the night before, on her way to the casino, where we all worked together. (Yes, I worked at a casino and had a gambling problem.) It was ironic that she delivered the news because there had been some run-ins at work between the two of them, where management had to get involved. It was all because of me.

I called Toi's mother as soon as I found out. She confirmed that she had died.

Reflecting on the night, I know I would have gone to her house had I not been high. Timing is everything. In my mind I kept thinking, *If I had asked to take her to work, or perhaps if I had been there, would it have changed her timeline in some kind of way and maybe she would still be alive?* I just didn't know.

Guilt and pain filled my head as I grasped what I had done... The last time I saw her I didn't even say goodbye. That night was weird. My addiction had robbed me, once again, of spending time with those I cared about.

And then I was questioning God again. Seven years prior, my son passed away and then my dad passed away. Then my fiancé, someone else I loved, passed away. I started to think *Am I this bad person, and is this the punishment or karma I have to deal with?*

At that point, that's when I decided I was going to leave Donna's apartment, and move to Indianapolis with my best friend – who had been trying to get me to move all along. I was excited to have a new start in a new environment.

Hoping for Closure

Toi had lost control of her car and hit a tree. The next time I went to Gary to visit, about a year after her accident, I went to that home. I felt led to go and hoped to get some closure, somehow. When I knocked on the family's door to get permission to spend time at the tree, I explained to the man of the house who I was and why I was there. He welcomed me and invited me inside to chat with his wife, explaining that he was on his way out to the grocery store. As if that wasn't odd enough, after a few moments, his wife and I went to the tree where she revealed that immediately after the accident she got into the car with Toi as they waited for the ambulance to come.

She told me. "I was doing what I could to comfort her, and I was sitting with her when she took her last breathe. I could tell she had a good spirit and I knew she was going to heaven."

She then told me that for many months to follow, people would come to that tree, as if it was a memorial site, and that they were moving soon.

I was quiet. I thanked her and left.

As I drove off I was feeling a sense of relief because I believed the lady and I believed Toi went to heaven. I just felt better. I didn't feel like my addiction had anything to do with her death anymore. I took that out of my mind, and never picked those thoughts back up.

Treatment of Women

The way I treated women was heavily influenced by what I saw.

- My treatment of women came from watching my stepdad and my friends with their girlfriends. On one hand I saw the verbal and physical abuse that was going on and on the other I saw what I thought looked like fun having more than one woman.

- More than one woman to me meant that I didn't have to deal with different attitudes if I didn't want to because I had options. I also believed that if I could do nice things for women they could do nice things for me, whether it was sexually or financially.

- I never thought I would be a man that would use a woman, take advantage of them or be addicted to the attention that I got from them. I realize now I was compensating for the fact that when I was in high school I wasn't really that popular and attractive guy that I wanted to be.

Gambling

When I started gambling in the beginning it was just something to do to pass time. I was trying to balance gambling and getting high at the same time. Little did I know that was a recipe for disaster. Because of the drugs, my relationship that I really wanted was failing and the continued gambling gave me an outlet to feel the void of what I did not have. I knew I was in bad shape when I went to the casino with NO money and saw myself in the mirror looking a hot mess. If I didn't know already that day I knew I was addicted to gambling and had a serious problem.

Today I'm looking back at the way I treated people and the way I dealt with women, gambling, and getting high. I thought God was really trying to get my attention. *Do people have to die for God to get my attention?* That's kind of big for me to think... but it's what I had wondered. I was struggling. I just wish things had been different.

> *"I really hoped God wasn't using my loved ones to reach me. For a short period, after moving out of Gary, I was regaining control, or so I thought."*

Budgeting Addictions

Getting my life back on track has been a long process. First, I had to believe I could and ask God for help. If He wouldn't have stepped in, I would probably still be on the street or in the ground. It took many years to get somewhat back on track, before I actually got to the place where I stopped getting high.

When I was getting high, deep down inside of me I knew it wasn't the life for me. After I was reintroduced to smoking primo joints again, I found myself deliberately taking breaks because when things looked too bad, I was more comfortable pulling back than embarrassing myself by "looking bad" to others. Somehow, I was able to pull back.

Priorities Are What We Make Them

I've always been conscious about my appearance and the way others saw me, therefore, I didn't want to start to look like I was strung out. At times, when I started losing weight because smoking primo joints takes away your appetite, I started wearing extra clothes to make me appear bigger than I was. I literally wore two pair of pants some days so it would make my weight loss less obvious.

I knew my deceased son and my two girls would not look up to "a crackhead" for a dad. When people think of "crackheads," we think of someone smoking from a pipe. I didn't ever do that, I laced my weed with crack and smoked it. It was a different feeling – one of calm and cool. A place of comfort and good feelings, a place to escape what was going on. It got to the point that I smoked when things went bad, and I smoked when things went good. I was high all the time – I liked the feeling and getting to that feeling became more important than anything else at those times. The high was different than a cocaine high or a straight "pipe" high. It was an intensified weed high which didn't give the munchies, took away my appetite and caused my smoking expense to go up times 10. So, no I wasn't "on the pipe" but anyone who smokes crack, in any form, is a crackhead.

I couldn't sustain the habit financially. The expense, coupled with my gambling habit, cost me dearly. For most of the seven years I served as a correctional officer, I didn't have a place of my own – I couldn't afford weed, crack, gambling, a car note and rent at the same time. Something had to go – and during those days especially, I was going from house to house, at times living with one of my sisters or one of the women I was dating. I was still wanting to "be free" and "be in control" and do what I wanted to do, at the expense of everything and everyone else. I often found myself dating several people at one time – I guess the variety made me feel empowered.

Although not having my own place was stressful in a way, not having to pay rent afforded me the luxury of feeding my habits, so I just went with it, though the eventual cost of my activities was extremely high.

Sometimes I would even mark on a calendar to keep up with the days I got high and how much money I spent so I could see exactly how much money I was spending. When I felt I was spending too much on getting high, I could and would "take a time out," purposely pulling back to regain my ability to balance whatever was going on at the time. It sounds odd, and it was, but I think it goes back to that part of me which knew this life wasn't, ultimately, for me.

I started to know I was lost yet I was helpless to do anything about it. It was as if I was trapped in a film, set in the casino, an invisible entity roaming about, fixated on feeding the addictions, alienated from anything and everything positive or good. That happened when I was hanging out in the casino with no money, disconnecting from people I normally communicated with, calling off work for various reasons, having cars repossessed and being evicted from my apartment. When I look back, it's kind of unbelievable to me. It's unbelievable because I'm not clouded by the addictions any longer. However, when I was getting high all the time, it was normal and I just took things day by day, figuring I could get another car, or get another job or get another woman, or live in a room or sleep on a couch until I could get another place. I always felt I was being logical and reasonable even though my life was completely out of control.

My addictions were attacking me in the area of drugs, gambling and women. I have shared more deeply about some of these already. Here's an overview of what getting to rock bottom looked like for me as a result of my choices:

LIST OF EVENTS/LOSSES

- 1994 Son drowns at beach (Chose to use weed + crack to elevate high/escape)
- 1996 Purchased a new car
- 1996 Broke up with my girlfriend (Was living with her so I had to move)
- 1996 Moved in with my sister
- 1997 Moved into my own apartment
- 1998 Second daughter born (Her mother was loyal, I was not)
- 1998 Car set on fire in my apartment parking lot (Dating multiple women)
- 1998 Purchased a new car
- 1998 Resigned from the prison/went to casino to work (Questionable drug test)
- 1999 Moved into an apartment with daughter's mom (Prioritizing getting high and gambling over paying bills and rent)
- 2000 Car repossessed

- 2000 Bought another car and moved in my own place
- 2001 In May father passed and car repossessed (Deeply hurt by his passing)
- 2001 In November My fiancé died in a car accident (Was high on her last night)
- 2001 Moved to Indy with my best friend (Left old job, new job, changed environment)
- 2002 Moved back to Gary (Lived with a relative)
- 2002 Started working back at the casino/moved back with daughter's mom (I had nowhere else to stay)
- 2003 Took income tax check to casino (Won money and purchased another car)
- 2003 Moved out and went to my sister's
- 2004 In June my sister moved and I knew she was tired of me getting high and trying to borrow money from her. I didn't move in with her and slept in my car for a few days and then moved in with my mom.
- 2004 July Lost job at casino and unemployed for 3 months (Called off too many times)
- 2004 October started working at furniture store (Saved my life)

- 2007 December moved to back to Indy to open new stores (Got serious about living addiction free)
- 2009 Stopped getting high and gambling (Got a bit better about dealing with women)

Just looking at that list is a lot for me. What do you think?

Getting Past the Fear

Sometimes we have to go through things for God to show us what we're here for. So that we can help other people go through what they are going through. We can't help other people go through things unless we've gone through it ourselves.

I was at a broken, depressed state. I've been sad, I've been mad, but I just knew that from my foundation, I think that was so important for my mom to take us to church because even though we were young, we were still in the house of God. It was just that I knew that God loved us, period, during my darkest moments and I knew that God loved me regardless. I could have been dead in several situations. But since he spared me I know I am to tell you that you can live. You have to treat people with kindness. I apologized to my ex-wife for leaving them and for treating her the way I did.

I was ego-centered. I just wanted to be seen a certain type of way. But on the inside I knew I was in a bad situation, a bad state. Getting high made me feel okay in the moment. Gambling and winning even for a moment just let me feel okay. And even if I lost, which you're going to lose more than you're going to win, the excitement of it gave me some sort of gratification. The thrill of even thinking if I win or lose it feels good – and anticipating winning, that put me in the frame of mind that I'll get to be big man on campus if I win.

With the addictions, the drug use and the gambling, I was searching for a feeling that I wasn't getting from my family or from my relationships, even knowing the consequences. The consequences didn't matter... my mom always told us "Pay your rent and pay your car note. If you have a job and you have a way to get there, you can pay your bills." So even after I was homeless and I started to work at the furniture store, I still kind of walked that line. At any moment, if I fell too far left, I would be in a bad situation. It could all be bad in an instant because of that line. And for me, when I go back, all the way back to the mid 90's, when I remember being in the bathroom of my son's grandmother's house, and I prayed, asking God to take it away from me. I held on through it all. I didn't know what He was going to do. But I knew he heard me and I know that God answers prayers.

So all the time when I was walking that line I was walking, and I could easily go left, I know it was God keeping me on that line, not allowing me to go left. I know He led me to change my environment as a first step – moving to Indianapolis. When we do pray and ask God to do something, we don't know what He's going to do but we must hold on to His promise that He is going to do – do something, in His time.

That's why I believe that I didn't try to go higher, I never tried to smoke crack by itself. The furniture store, at which I worked, really saved my life.

When I think about the two years that I continued to go back and forth, I think that was a spiritual struggle. Are you sure you want to leave this life over here? Are you sure you are done with this life? Are you sure you don't want to feel like this anymore? I had to make a decision. Just looking at the blessings over my life, and how I knew that I could have been dead. One of the guys I used to buy from, people ran into his house to rob him, and they killed him. I thought of the countless times that I would go wherever he told me to meet him. I don't think God loved me more than he loved him, I just think that God's protection was over my life. I couldn't go back. I couldn't go back to that lifestyle knowing how God had protected and blessed me.

Getting away to Indianapolis, and into a career where I could excel, be productive, make money, look good, and begin to truly feel good about myself saved my life, by His grace and mercy – it just took me a bit to catch up, buy in and allow Him to do His good works in me – breaking me. Breaking my habits, breaking my addictions and breaking through to His goodness and spirit in me – awakening me to what he had for me all along.

Once I made that decision, I believe God knew he could trust me with money. My income increased each year over the next three years, actually, one year it increased over $30,000 from one year to the next because He knew he could trust me with money. I haven't looked back since then. Using drugs, getting high hasn't been a thought since that night in the hotel room when I hit rock bottom.

Everybody Has Their Own Journey

I believe that everybody's journey is their journey. Some people may need to go to rehab, and that's great for them. I just didn't have to do it. Some people may need counseling. I think my "rehab" was based on my spirituality, and removing myself from the environment. Though I could have come to Indianapolis to find connections, I didn't. Once God takes something away, it's taken away – when we submit. When I submitted to His will for my life, I began to live. For me it took 40 years to give into to God and His will, to submit to His will for my life.

When I think about the fact that some of the situations I found myself in, when I think about how God is allowing me to live my life right now, when I read Psalm 86 and I know that he hears us and answers our prayers, and that he loves us in spite of ourselves, it makes me thankful and makes me cry. When I think about my mom, and her still being here, I'm grateful. I want her to be proud of her son. When I think about the relationship I have with the mothers of my children today, in spite of all I did, when I look at the change in my life, conscious decisions and changes I made, that I had control of ... in sales, we always say, "Control what you can control." I am grateful.

Looking Into the Mirror

When you look in the mirror and can say to yourself, "You are a good person. Yeah, you made some mistakes. Everybody makes mistakes." But you own it and take responsibility for it and you choose to move forward, that's where the rewards are.

If you sit in that space, judging or feeling ashamed or sorry for yourself, continuing to sit in that space, that's when you go back to whatever that was that made you feel better when you were in that space.

Am I being arrogant or self-centered to think that my son had to die for me to listen to God? I certainly hope not – yet as I struggled with that question for 20 years, it continually put me back into a place of guilt.

Before I smoked my first joint I saw others smoking and they looked cool and seemed to feel good after they did it. It made me curious and want to do it too. When I got high the first time, I loved the feeling and I was hooked on feeling good. And as a 14 year old, it made me feel cool. There wasn't much more to it than that, in my head as a teenager. However, my desire to be cool and feel good started to make things easier when adult things started happening in my life, like becoming a father at 17 years old. At some point, even though I didn't recognize it, getting high became a crutch or a way of coping with life, stress and anything I didn't feel comfortable dealing with. I'm not sure when it became an actual addiction but I do know that for whatever reasons the 17-year experience, though it seemed hell, gave me the opportunity to now help others and maybe lessen their struggles. I didn't recognize addictions were holding me back – a weight lifted off of me, feeling like you can breathe again – and then at some point you may say wow, that's all it took? Or, it feels so good, why I didn't let it go sooner… and then eventually, you feel proud of yourself for doing it – your own personal moment where you may even be in a room full of people, but inside, by yourself, you are proud of yourself. Getting there is possible, as long as you don't give up.

Once I Made that Decision

When I think about the gambling and all the money I lost, and all the money I spent on drugs, for me to help somebody, I look at money a little different because I wasted money in those two areas. I want to help people now, financially. My relationship with money is different to me today. Money is a resource but God is the Source. I've also learned that when I focus on the Source, the money will come. So yes, I wasted a lot, but no more.

You have to be honest with yourself. You can't sugarcoat your situation. You have to know where you are in it. You can't know where you're going unless you know where you're at. Sometimes we think we're strong enough to deal with things on our own. Some things people can help us with. Some things only God can help us with.

I had to forgive myself for the way I acted.

3 Steps to Forgiveness

1. You have to ask God for forgiveness.
2. You have to ask God to help you forgive you.
3. You have to ask others to forgive you.

When I think about the people who overdose on drugs, *What's the difference between them and me?* I don't know personally anybody who has overdosed, but I've been in those hotel rooms by myself so I can picture that moment, when perhaps they want to be alone, I get that. I don't think anybody starts off mixing cocaine and heroin starting at the gate... I do know that it's a progression and I believe it's a getaway.... That's why they are at a hotel room by themselves, it's a getaway. I believe something in their life, and it doesn't matter how much money or fame a person has, something, whatever they were dealing with, I don't think they had gotten to the point where they could ask for forgiveness... to ask God for forgiveness, to forgive themselves, or to ask others to forgive them. So I think those overdoses are somehow connected to those moments.

This psalm is my way of praising and worshipping God. I want Him to know that I love Him, I need Him, I can't do anything without Him, and I pray that He hears my prayers all the days of my life.

Psalm 86 New International Version (NIV)

Psalm 86

A Prayer of David.

¹ Hear me, Lord, and answer me,
    for I am poor and needy.
² Guard my life, for I am faithful to you;
    save your servant who trusts in you.
You are my God; ³ have mercy on me, Lord,
    for I call to you all day long.
⁴ Bring joy to your servant, Lord,
    for I put my trust in you.

⁵ You, Lord, are forgiving and good,
    abounding in love to all who call to you.
⁶ Hear my prayer, Lord;
    listen to my cry for mercy.
⁷ When I am in distress, I call to you,
    because you answer me.

⁸ Among the gods there is none like you, Lord;
    no deeds can compare with yours.
⁹ All the nations you have made
    will come and worship before you, Lord;
    they will bring glory to your name.

¹⁰ For you are great and do marvelous deeds;
   you alone are God.

¹¹ Teach me your way, Lord,
   that I may rely on your faithfulness;
give me an undivided heart,
   that I may fear your name.
¹² I will praise you, Lord my God, with all my heart;
   I will glorify your name forever.
¹³ For great is your love toward me;
   you have delivered me from the depths,
   from the realm of the dead.

¹⁴ Arrogant foes are attacking me, O God;
   ruthless people are trying to kill me—
   they have no regard for you.
¹⁵ But you, Lord, are a compassionate and gracious God,
   slow to anger, abounding in love and faithfulness.
¹⁶ Turn to me and have mercy on me;
   show your strength in behalf of your servant;
save me, because I serve you
   just as my mother did.
¹⁷ Give me a sign of your goodness,
   that my enemies may see it and be put to shame,
   for you, Lord, have helped me and comforted me.

Making the Transition

I made a transition from arrogance to humility. A lot of times people say there is a thin line between arrogance and confidence. It is, but the difference is about the source – arrogance comes from (insecurity/our flesh, just us personally, trying to appear a certain way "puffed up") confidence/humility comes from (inner knowing/the Lord).

> *"Arrogant foes are attacking me, O God; ruthless people are trying to kill me—*
> *they have no regard for you."* Psalm 86:14

At first I didn't understand it because I was thinking no one was personally trying to kill me. But when I think about wanting to get away from what was happening in my life, it was easier to escape into the addictions that took me to a place where I could feel okay. So the arrogant foes attacking me and the ruthless people trying to kill me were really me – the part of me who was disconnected from God. My inner turmoil kept me searching for something – comfort… killing my spirit, killing my manhood, bringing me down, killing who I thought I was, attempting to murder my purpose.

Old School Advice From Mr. Bud

My coworker, Mr. Bud, told me that there's an art to management. You always want to hug them first, then slug them whenever they're doing wrong, and then hug them again. Hug 'em (praise them), slug 'em (give feedback about what's not working), then hug 'em (praise them) again really does work, and I had to work on the hug 'em/praise part because they would say I was strict and unapproachable. I was sluggin' all the time. It took about two years to get that stigma of being unapproachable off of me. But it didn't just come off. I worked on that. I just changed my delivery and wanted to bring out the best in people. But I realized you can't bring out the best in people by always telling them what they did wrong. And you can't bring out the best in you when you're always condemning yourself telling yourself how wrong you are but not taking steps to figure out how right you can be. At least I thought I was regaining control. I thought that's what would save me, my willpower.

Regaining control! That's what I was trying to do, but wasn't that part of the problem? I thought I could do it, control myself and my actions, but I wasn't done with my addictions yet. I hadn't turned my addictions, control or life over to the One who ultimately had the power to change me.

Know This

Your life is worth living. Your life has value. You have something to offer to someone. Your story of how you got to where you got can help somebody. You are stronger than what you think or what you know. As long as you are alive, you have an opportunity to change and to make things better. You have to believe in yourself in order for others to believe in you. Don't give up or quit on yourself. Trust the gifts you have and if you don't know, ask God to help you find out what they are. If you can't do it for yourself, do it for your children or family – and if you don't have any children or family, find a reason to live. If you think you've tried everything and you haven't gone to God with your situation, I would say, try God.

Are You Due for A Change?

"Living the life you and others can be proud of takes a few things, including courage, admitting when things are bad, discovering purpose, finding strength and having endurance, especially when you know you're at the end of your rope."

The Reason I Didn't Go to Rehab

It's not that I didn't need to go to rehab...

I always knew that rehab was an option but I was too embarrassed to go. I didn't want to face what others would have thought about me had I gone. Going seemed more horrific than dealing with it myself. But let me be clear, that strength came from the core of me, not from the addicted me.

Several times during those 17 years I had asked God to take the addictions away from me and help me heal. When I hit rock bottom I knew where to turn. At that point, I was ready to accept the healing.

I made a decision to take it one day at a time, to understand I wanted and want a better life for myself. It's not like it's all said and done and I'm "cured." No, I'm still dealing with issues as they come up. However, I don't turn to my previous addictions to make me feel better.

Knowing that what I did then doesn't align with the life I'm living now, it's easier to not be tempted. I've incorporated more meaningful activities in my life and I purposefully don't have as much free time. Also, I am acutely aware of my environment. I don't go to places where people are getting high. I do go to places which feed my spirit. I also read daily, filling my mind with positive ideas and thoughts.

Every day I remember where I was, knowing that I don't want to go back to that dark place. That's incentive to *Get Back Up*. And I rely on my faith in God and the relationship I've built with Him to make it through every challenge.

Decisions and Consequences

Small decisions ended up with big consequences because of the path I chose. What about you? Today I challenge you to stand as **A Vision of Excellence**. It may take some work to get there but it's possible if you apply yourself. It's all about vision and applying yourself.

If you see someone succeeding, you don't have to envy them or try to take what's theirs. You can have your own success. Just apply yourself, and that starts with acknowledging what may be holding you back. Fear often holds us back. That fear is often based on the past and freely runs around in our heads, complicating life and causing us to settle for less than who we are and for less than who we were born to be.

Be mindful of your triggers. Some triggers will try and tug you backward while others will do just the opposite – serving as constant reminders of what you don't want.

When I get frustrated I tend to want to clam up and stop talking. That can come out as being harsh and cold. That's not my intention. But it's one of the ways I learned to cope and deal with life. It's a natural place to go because I don't want to say something I have to come back and apologize for because I feel like people don't forget. People love to say, "I forgive you," but they don't forget it. Therefore, I think people, myself included, find it hard to forgive. I don't want to offend or yell, I want to be nice, most of the time.

I don't want to yell at anyone. It's because I used to try and force people to talk or do what I wanted them to do, but that doesn't work and I've lost meaningful relationships as a result.

I don't want to go back and forth. Therefore, to avoid it, I either shut down or I want to do something – that's been my pattern and I'm working on and through it. Once I understood how important it was to really allow myself to be vulnerable to the point where I wasn't trying to mask anything, especially the way I felt, I was willing to let my feelings/emotions flow, and then the negativity and darkness made way for light and understanding. I'm a man in progress with *A Vision of Excellence* allowing me to *Get Back Up*.

Tired of Being Tired

We are all works in progress, and are fortunate to have brand new opportunities to change our thinking, feelings and habits for the better. One of the best things to do is to identify your triggers/obstacles and frustrations. Over time some frustrations built up and caused me to desire to change. If you can relate to any of them, perhaps they can serve as motivation to propel you to keep moving forward, especially during difficult times…

1. I got tired of being broke and living pay check to pay check.
2. I was tired of how I felt in the morning after getting high the night before.
3. I was definitely frustrated with my weight loss.
4. I was tired of being paranoid about people knowing and talking about me behind my back.
5. I was tired of living with people, and moving from place to place.
6. I was tired of trying to borrow money a couple of days after payday, trying to pay for gas, after the pay check ran out, gambling.

7. I was tired of being tired and I knew I wasn't living the life that I wanted.

If you can agree, I challenge you to write your own list of frustrations and then choose to acknowledge and overcome them every single day.

Change Takes Work

One of the biggest challenges to change is fear. There are many acronyms for FEAR but one of the funniest ones I've heard is "Forget Everything And Run!" I love that! If only life were that simple! I've found that fear often "attacks" when we are striving to live life, and especially when we are working on ourselves (Change and Personal Development).

Six Areas Where Fear Often Attaches

1. Fear of the Unknown
2. Fear of Failure
3. Fear of Success
4. Fear of Commitment
5. Fear of Disapproval
6. Fear of Financial Security

If you recognize that you've attached yourself to fear, instead of trying to "Forget Everything and Run," you get to stand up and tell yourself you are greater than that four letter word and then do something about it. A positive attitude is necessary, but it's just the start – you must also do something!

Change Is a Process

Way before I started my personal development company, ANDO (Ambition, Nutrition, Dedication, Occupation, which promotes Bright Futures), I was living in an extremely dark place. When I literally lost everything, I had to choose to do something different, make big changes, get over my fears and move forward by stepping out on faith.

Can you relate to being held back by fear? Well, I'm here to tell you that standing in *A Vision of Excellence* is a much better path than Forgetting Everything and Running!

Being scared of change locks you right where you are. Don't be scared. My hope is that you live in strength through your struggles.

Strength through Struggles

1. **You are not your failures.**

    Often times we get held down and discouraged because we continue to live in our past and beat ourselves up over past mistakes and failures. We should learn from our mistakes/failures and keep moving forward.

    Moving forward means believing in yourself, setting new goals and working toward those goals by creating a plan of action and working that plan. Because you are doing something new, moving forward also means trying new things, learning new skills and being mentored/coached to success if and when necessary. Your mindset, attitude and altitude are determined by your willingness to break through to your potentialities.

2. **Paint a transformation picture.**

    There are steps to success and they are not necessarily gigantic or difficult. If you've been in addiction, you may not know what "normal" life looks like so creating new habits will help you transform your life.

    One of the most important elements of transformation is consistency, along with vision. It also means finding and maintaining sustainable work which pays your bills and which you find fulfilling. Taking care of your health, creating (healthy) daily routines, working, earning a living, saving, having a comfortable place to live, extracurricular activities, community service, attending church and interacting with people, especially loved ones are examples of routines which will support your success.

    When you contribute you feel better and so do the people around you.

3. **You have a responsibility to your family.**

   As the oldest, my siblings looked up to me for guidance and support. The truth is, for many years I was not present to offer either. If I could change the past I would. However, that's not possible.

   We can't take back what happened but we can be determined not to go back to the same behavior.

   Your life matters and so does your presence. Your family may be biological or not. Whatever the case, they depend on you for different things at different times.

   Personal issues come up and life is challenging. Part of being in a healthy relationship is sharing the good, the bad and the ugly. Learning to work through day to day challenges together is paramount to living a whole life, because isolation and martyrdom keep you closed and mentally drained. You owe it to your family and to yourself to be healthy, willing and available to be dependable, present and connected. Engagement, showing love and active involvement keeps everyone vibrant and together.

4. **Choose to make sound decisions.**

   Don't repeat bad decisions which create bad outcomes. You may feel at times your hands are tied, but your hands are never tied. Think, "Is this going to help me or hurt me?" "Will this decision set me up for success or set me back?" Stand by the decisions you make. Be honest with yourself, you won't always make the right choices but taking time to focus on the best and worst case scenarios will help steer you in the right direction.

You have to make the decision to want to do and be better every single day, all day. Think about your options and the consequences of each choice, and then make your sound decision.

When you change how you think and process your thoughts, that's when you begin to change your life for the better. Practice making small, good decisions quickly. This will get you into the habit of thinking before you act and will build a foundation for sound decision-making as a part of your daily routine.

6 Daily Steps to Maintain Progress

1. I wake up every day and open my blinds to let the light in.
2. I am thankful for another day.
3. I remind myself of who I am, and that I am a winner.
4. I remind myself that today is one step closer to accomplishing my goals and aspirations.

5. I make a conscious decision to do my best today and every day no matter what.

6. I am aware of how I treat people and I keep a positive attitude to make it through each situation.

Affirmation

"I know where I came from. I know where I am. I know where I'd like to go. I also know that going backward is not an option for me. I choose to see myself as A Vision of Excellence and I choose to Get Back Up any and every time I feel down."

Hopefully, by peeking into my journey you will be motivated, inspired and empowered to get past any attachments which may be impeding you from standing in *A Vision of Excellence* because I want you to *Be Proud of Yourself*. As I mentioned before, it takes effort and applying yourself. If I can do it, you can too! Trust and believe that.

About the Author

Author Greg Goodman empowers people to believe in themselves, to overcome adversity and to stand up when feeling knocked down. As a top sales leader for over 15 years, he knows, from experience, how to be successful despite the obstacles and empowers others to do the same. As an advocate and mentor of young men, his message focuses on self-worth, achievement and success.

In *A Vision of Excellence*, **Author Greg Goodman** shares his personal story of adversity mixed with terrible choices and horrible consequences, only to find victory in the end, after choosing to *Get Back Up*.

Greg Goodman says, "You can be at your worst and stay down. Or you can *Get Back Up* if you're willing to put in the work to change what you feel, what you're doing and see yourself differently. No matter what you've been through or what you've done, today is the day to believe in yourself and see a better future."

www.ingramcontent.com/pod-product-compliance
Lightning Source LLC
Chambersburg PA
CBHW050446010526
44118CB00013B/1699